Original title:
Lingering Light

Copyright © 2024 Creative Arts Management OÜ
All rights reserved.

Author: Samuel Kensington
ISBN HARDBACK: 978-9916-90-676-7
ISBN PAPERBACK: 978-9916-90-677-4

Softly Fading Horizons

In twilight's gentle, warm embrace,
The sun dips low, begins to trace.
Colors swirl in soft retreat,
Where day and night so softly meet.

Whispers of winds, a fading tune,
Moonlight dances, like a boon.
Stars awaken, shyly gleam,
Painting shadows in the dream.

The world slows down, takes a breath,
In quietude, defying death.
Every sigh a note of peace,
In this stillness, worries cease.

Softly fading, horizons blend,
A tranquil space where hearts amend.
In this twilight, magic flows,
Embracing all, as daylight goes.

A Soft Departure into the Night

The sun slips low, a gentle sigh,
Whispers of dusk draw near to cry.
Stars awaken, twinkling bright,
In the embrace of tender night.

Shadows dance on silent streets,
As moonlight's kiss the world entreats.
Softly drift, the dreams take flight,
A soft departure into the night.

Nostalgic Shades of the Eventide

Golden hues in fading light,
Memories bloom from day to night.
Whispers of laughter, days gone by,
In the fading warmth, I sigh.

Beneath the trees where shadows grow,
Echoes of ages long ago.
The heart recalls with tender pride,
Nostalgic shades of the eventide.

Whispers from the Starlit Veil

In the depths of velvet skies,
Whispers float like silent sighs.
Glimmers dance on cosmic seas,
Carried softly by the breeze.

Voices of the night conspire,
Secrets born from distant fire.
Wrapped in dreams, we close our eyes,
Whispers from the starlit veil arise.

Murmurs of a Sinking Horizon

The sun dips low, a fiery glance,
Clouds ablaze, in evening's dance.
As shadows stretch and colors blend,
Murmurs of a day will end.

Oceans sigh beneath the glow,
In twilight's grip, soft winds will blow.
Horizons sink, as day concedes,
Murmurs of a sinking horizon, hearts freed.

Notes from the Dimming Hour

Whispers linger in the air,
As daylight softly fades away.
Secrets held in shadows there,
Nighttime starts to find its sway.

Stars begin their silent rise,
Painting skies with distant light.
Each note sung, a soft surprise,
Echoes through the velvet night.

Celestial Shadows Dance

Beneath the moon's enchanting glow,
Silent figures twirl and sway.
In the dark, their secrets flow,
Guided by the night's ballet.

Stars above with twinkling eyes,
Watch the rhythm of their grace.
Time dissolves as twilight sighs,
A dance lost in endless space.

The Gold That Melts Away

Golden rays of sunbeam light,
Drip like honey through the leaves.
Closing in, the coming night,
Softly weaves what daylight weaves.

In the dusk, the shimmer fades,
Treasures turn to shadows deep.
What once shone, the twilight trades,
For the secrets twilight keeps.

Sands of Time in Dimming Glow

Sands of time slip through the hand,
Each grain holds a fleeting dream.
In the dusk, the moments stand,
Glowing soft like silver steam.

As the twilight calls us near,
Memories in whispers flow.
In the hour, we find the clear,
Pieces lost in dimming glow.

Celestial Dimming

Stars flicker in the fading light,
Night unfolds its velvet cloak.
The moon whispers to the night,
As shadows begin to evoke.

Whispers dance on cooling air,
The sky bleeds hues of blue.
As daylight slips without a care,
The cosmos starts anew.

The Whisper of the Horizon

Where sky meets sea in gentle sighs,
The world dissolves in gold and gray.
A soft call from the sunlit skies,
Where dreams and daylight play.

Waves reflect a fading glow,
The horizon blushes bright.
In tranquil moments, feelings flow,
As day surrenders night.

Hidden Colors of Dusk's Breath

In dusk's embrace, tones softly blend,
Coral and violet fiercely play.
Time whispers secrets without end,
As light begins to decay.

A canvas rich with stories told,
Brush strokes gentle and profound.
Nature's art, a sight to behold,
As dusk spins round and round.

An Ode to Dimensional Hues

In every shade, a tale resides,
Colors merge, creating space.
Life's spectrum, a journey wide,
Reflecting love's warm embrace.

Each layer tells of moments passed,
A tapestry of night and day.
In colors bright, shadows are cast,
As dimensions glide away.

The Twilight of Hope's Dreams

In the hush of fading light,
Dreams begin to take their flight.
Voices whisper soft and low,
In the twilight, hopes still glow.

Shadows gather, stars appear,
Fading doubts, we hold them dear.
Moments linger, softly fade,
In this twilight, dreams are made.

Glowing Trails of the Setting Sun

Golden hues paint the sky,
As the day begins to die.
Trails of light dance in the night,
Glowing softly, pure delight.

Whispers float on evening's breeze,
Nature's sigh among the trees.
Each sunset brings a promise new,
In the dusk, our dreams break through.

The Dance of Faint Stars

In the velvet of the night,
Stars awaken, shining bright.
Faintly twinkling, they engage,
In a cosmic, silent stage.

With each flicker, stories told,
Of lost dreams and hearts so bold.
In this dance of light and dark,
Hope ignites with every spark.

Memories Cloaked in Dusk

As the day begins to close,
Memories blend like fragrant prose.
Cloaked in dusk, they softly weave,
Tales of joy that we believe.

Every moment lingers here,
Wrapped in shadows, ever near.
In the silence, past and now,
Dusk reveals the sacred vow.

Fading Echoes of Dusk

Softly fades the light of day,
Whispers dance on shadows' play.
Colors bleed into the night,
Stars awaken, dreams take flight.

Where the twilight meets the air,
Silence drapes, a gentle care.
Memories linger, sweet and brief,
In this moment, find relief.

Echoes of the sun retreat,
Nature's pulse, a steady beat.
With each breath, we slow our pace,
In the dusk, we find our place.

Whispers of the Setting Sun

Golden hues begin to blend,
Horizon's edge, the day must end.
Birds call out in evening's light,
As the sky turns shades of night.

Whispers soft as shadows creep,
Promises the twilight keeps.
In this hour, dreams softly form,
Wrapped in dusk, embrace the warm.

Light retreats with grace and ease,
Gentle whispers in the breeze.
Nature holds her breath in peace,
In this moment, all will cease.

Shadows of the Day

Shadows stretch across the ground,
In the twilight, calm is found.
Echoes of the day's bright glare,
Fade into the evening air.

Coolness drapes the world in hush,
As the colors start to blush.
Fleeting moments, fleeting light,
In the balance of the night.

Time slips by, a soft embrace,
Day bows down, a graceful space.
In the silence, thoughts collide,
In the shadows, dreams reside.

Twilight's Gentle Embrace

Twilight whispers, softly speaks,
In the stillness, heartache seeks.
Tender moments start to blend,
As the day begins to end.

Stars ignite in velvet skies,
Glimmers dance like fireflies.
In that glow, we find our way,
Through the night, come what may.

Hope lies cradled in the dark,
As dreams ignite a tiny spark.
Feel the warmth of twilight's grace,
In its arms, we find our place.

Hints of Light in Stillness

In the quiet night, stars gleam,
Whispers of dreams gently stream.
Moonbeams dance on the serene lake,
Each reflection a promise to make.

Branches sway with tales untold,
Secrets of the night unfold.
A soft breeze carries the sigh,
Hints of light as shadows fly.

Memories Adrift in Twilight

Lost moments drift in the dusk,
Soft echoes linger, a gentle husk.
Faded laughter, a tender caress,
In twilight's embrace, we find our rest.

Ghosts of the past dance in the haze,
Each flicker a song of distant days.
The heart holds close what the mind forgets,
In this twilight, the light begets.

The Golden Echo of Dusk

The sun bows low, a golden hue,
Whispers of day bid the night adieu.
Crickets sing as shadows blend,
In dusk's embrace, the world does mend.

Amber skies fade into deep blue,
Every moment a memory true.
Time lingers softly, a fleeting hush,
In the silence, we feel the rush.

A Canvas Stained with Glow

Brush strokes of twilight paint the sky,
Swirls of color, a vibrant sigh.
Each hue a story, a tale untold,
A canvas stained with dreams of gold.

Stars begin to pierce the night's veil,
Guiding wanderers on their trail.
Artistry woven in the night air,
A canvas of light, a world laid bare.

Dusk's Gentle Lament

Whispers of twilight kiss the air,
Soft shadows dance without a care.
The sun dips low, a dying flame,
In silence, dusk calls out your name.

Each star awakens, shy and bright,
Cradled gently, the cloak of night.
Sighs of the past float on the breeze,
In the heart's stillness, we find our ease.

Memories linger, like faded light,
Songs of the day fade into night.
With every heartbeat, dusk will stay,
A gentle whisper to end our day.

The Interval Between Day and Night

A canvas painted with orange hues,
The sun bids farewell, with soft adieu.
Birds find perches, hush their songs,
As shadows stretch and night prolongs.

In this stillness, time bends and sways,
Caught in the magic of twilight's gaze.
Day and night hold a breathless truce,
In this liminal space, souls deduce.

With fireflies blinking, the world ignites,
Hopeful glimmers through tranquil nights.
In every heartbeat, a promise lies,
The dance of dusk under indigo skies.

Colors that Fade like Secrets

Petals drop softly from a tired bloom,
Colors that whisper, fade into gloom.
Once vivid dreams, now muted tone,
Echoes of laughter, once brightly shone.

Secrets woven in twilight's thread,
Crimson memories dance with the dead.
Each hue a story, drowned in the night,
Splashes of joy, now out of sight.

As night blankets over fading grace,
Shadows engulf what time can't trace.
Colors that fade, but never cease,
In twilight's embrace, we find our peace.

Echoes Carved in Dusk's Embrace

Footsteps echo on cobbled stone,
Each whisper lingers, never alone.
In the dusk, stories softly untwine,
Carved in the silence, a love divine.

Moonlight bathes in silver streams,
Cradling the night like cherished dreams.
Voices of dusk, they call and play,
In tender moments, we drift away.

With every heartbeat, the world aligns,
Echoes of laughter in starry designs.
Remembered in shadows, time can't erase,
Lives intertwined in dusk's warm embrace.

A Filter of Fading Warmth

Beneath the fading sun,
Leaves whisper soft goodbyes.
A gentle breeze doth run,
Through branches steeped in sighs.

Moments drift like dust,
Caught in twilight's embrace.
Memories are a must,
As time begins to race.

Shadows stretch and play,
On paths we used to tread.
In the end of day,
The warmth no longer led.

Yet in the quiet air,
A promise lingers near.
Of hearts that used to care,
Still whispering, still clear.

The Edge Between Light and Shadow

At dawn the shadows flee,
As light begins to swell.
A dance of mystery,
In the quiet knell.

Where twilight dips its brush,
The worlds collide and blend.
In harmony they hush,
Both light and dark, my friend.

The border's softly drawn,
In hues of gold and gray.
With every draping dawn,
We find our truth at play.

In this fragile space,
We navigate our dreams.
Embracing each embrace,
The edge that softly gleams.

The Soft Quality of Goodbye.

In whispers through the trees,
The end is softly breathed.
A tender, wistful ease,
As hearts become unweaved.

Each word hangs in the air,
Like dew on morning grass.
A moment, lost in care,
As time begins to pass.

The eyes that speak of pain,
Yet shine with love's last light.
In sorrow's sweet refrain,
We find our strength to fight.

Goodbyes are just a door,
To paths we cannot see.
With each farewell, we soar,
Into eternity.

Whispers of the Twilight Glow

The twilight paints the skies,
In shades of softest gold.
As daylight gently dies,
Its secrets to unfold.

A hush falls o'er the land,
Where shadows start to swell.
In silence, hand in hand,
We weave a timeless spell.

The stars begin to wink,
With promises untold.
In every breath we think,
We'll chase the night so bold.

Whispers fill the night air,
A lullaby of dreams.
In twilight's softest care,
Reality redeems.

Shadows Embrace the Horizon

As the sun begins to wane,
Shadows stretch across the land.
Whispers dance on twilight's breath,
Cradled by night's gentle hand.

Soft hues blend with fading light,
The horizon swallows day.
Silent secrets held in dusk,
As the world slips away.

Stars awaken one by one,
Painting dreams in the sky.
Moonlight bathes the quiet earth,
As time begins to sigh.

In this magical embrace,
Time stands still, a fleeting grace.
Night unfolds its velvet chair,
Wrapping all in tender care.

Echoes of the Dusk Flame

Flickers dance upon the night,
As shadows weave 'round the flame.
Echoes whisper tales untold,
And the darkness calls my name.

The day melts into memory,
In hues of purple and gold.
Each moment slips, a fleeting breath,
As the night's embrace unfolds.

Crimson embers softly glow,
Sparks of dreams lost in flight.
In this world of quiet dreams,
The dusk holds secrets tight.

Embrace the fading heartbeat,
Listen to the whispered song.
In the echoes of the flame,
We find where we belong.

Threads of a Fading Day

Threads of light begin to fray,
Weaving on a canvas grey.
Colors bleed into the night,
As the sun bids its goodbyes.

Whispers of the evening breeze,
Carry tales of joys and woes.
Fading footprints walk in time,
As the silken twilight grows.

Each moment softly drifts away,
Into shadows, soft as lace.
The tapestry of twilight folds,
Enfolding all in its embrace.

Gather dreams like autumn leaves,
Let them dance upon the air.
In the stillness, find your heart,
And hold the echoes sweeter there.

The Afterglow of Memory

In the afterglow we dwell,
Carved in light, a sacred spell.
Memories linger like a breeze,
Softly speaking, timeless tales.

Faded images resist the dark,
Filling hearts with warmth and light.
Each recall, a gentle spark,
Guiding us through the night.

Time erodes but does not erase,
The laughter shared, the warmth embraced.
In twilight's glow, we find our place,
With memories that time can't chase.

So let the echoes gently flow,
Embrace the warmth of what we know.
In the afterglow, we find our peace,
As moments weave their sweet release.

Whispers of Fading Color

In gardens where the petals fall,
The hues of spring begin to pall.
Soft sighs of twilight brush the leaves,
As nature whispers, gently grieves.

The canvas fades from bright to gray,
As daylight bids its sweet decay.
Each whisper carried on the breeze,
Reminds us time is meant to tease.

The golden rays now shy away,
While shadows stretch and softly play.
A palette dimmed, but still so fair,
In silence wraps the evening air.

Traces of Light's Departure

With every sunset's crimson glow,
The daylight bids a warm adieu.
Soft beams retreat, a gentle flight,
As darkness claims the edge of night.

The horizon blushes, then it sighs,
As stars awake in velvety skies.
Whispers linger in the air,
Of moments lost, a quiet prayer.

Each fading ray, a fleeting dream,
In twilight's arms, they gently beam.
The world transforms as shadows creep,
In dusk's embrace, the secrets keep.

Twilight's Poetic Breath

Beneath the arch of dusky skies,
The world transforms, and silence lies.
Each fleeting breath, a soft refrain,
Of lingering light, of gentle pain.

The stars ignite in twilight's kiss,
A whispered promise, fleeting bliss.
Each moment held in twilight's care,
Bears memories time cannot spare.

The dance of dusk, a fleeting glance,
Invites the night to join the dance.
In shadows deep, our hopes arise,
As twilight's breath ignites our skies.

A Lullaby of Dimming Day

The sun dips low beyond the hill,
A lullaby, the air is still.
Crickets sing, a soothing tune,
As day concedes to fading moon.

The clouds embrace the dusk's soft fold,
In hues of silver, pink, and gold.
Each note a tender warmth bestowed,
As nature hums the evening's ode.

With every sigh, the light departs,
Yet lingers still in quiet hearts.
A melody of dusk's delight,
As shadows dance with coming night.

Velvet Moments of Dusk

The sky wraps in hues of deep blue,
Stars awaken, a shimmering crew.
Whispers of night dance on the breeze,
Velvet moments bring hearts to ease.

Shadows stretch long as the sun dips low,
Crickets begin their nighttime show.
The world hushed, in soft-spoken grace,
In twilight's embrace, we find our place.

Soft glows linger where light meets dark,
Nature's canvas leaves its mark.
In these moments, we pause and reflect,
Savoring time, as dreams intersect.

With each heartbeat, the night moves near,
In velvet moments, we conquer fear.
Finding solace in the gentle night,
As dusk unfolds, our spirits take flight.

The Glow Before the Dark

A warm glow kisses the edge of sight,
As day surrenders to the coming night.
Sunset hues paint the clouds like fire,
Filling our hearts with a quiet desire.

Fingers of light stretch, then withdraw,
With every breath, the world feels raw.
The horizon blurs, gold meets grey,
In the glow before night claims the day.

The whispers of wind serenade the trees,
As twilight murmurs, carrying ease.
Every shadow grows, soft and stark,
In the gentle hush, we find our spark.

Moments linger, suspended with grace,
In twilight's warmth, we embrace space.
The glow whispers secrets, timeless and bright,
Before the deep stillness of approaching night.

Surrender to the Evening

Glistening stars break night's soft veil,
As solace settles on every trail.
We surrender to the evening's call,
In its tender hold, we quietly fall.

Moonlight weaves through branches high,
Casting dreams on the lullaby.
Silhouettes dance in a gentle sway,
Inviting us all to drift away.

The fragrance of night blooms sweet and rare,
Wrapping us in a fragrant affair.
Every sigh whispers stories untold,
As the evening embraces, both warm and bold.

Softly we linger, lost in its charms,
Welcoming the night, wrapped in its arms.
In surrendering time, our fears retreat,
As the evening unfolds, all hearts meet.

Resplendent Ghosts of Day's End

As shadows steal across the land,
Day's colors fade like grains of sand.
Resplendent ghosts of light take flight,
Woven in whispers of soft twilight.

Echoes of laughter drift on the air,
Memories linger, nestled in care.
Stories are told in the twilight glow,
As time moves gently, steady, and slow.

Chasing the day into night's soft fold,
Moments cherished, treasures untold.
Through the twilight, our spirits blend,
In the silence where day meets its end.

With every heartbeat, the stars arise,
Painting the night with wondrous ties.
Resplendent ghosts remind us of light,
As we dance together through the night.

Glinting Wishes of Twilight

Soft whispers in the air,
As daylight starts to fade.
Stars begin their gentle dance,
In twilight's serenade.

Shadows stretch and curl,
The sky dons a purple veil.
Each glimmer holds a secret,
Of dreams that softly sail.

The moon smiles in the deep,
As the world slows its pace.
Hopes ignite like fireflies,
In this enchanted space.

With every fleeting moment,
The night unveils its grace.
Glinting wishes in the dark,
Leave behind a trace.

Breath of the Coming Night

A hush falls over fields,
As sun bows to the land.
The breath of night awakens,
In shadows soft and grand.

Crickets serenade the dusk,
In a dance of sweet delight.
Cool winds carry whispers,
Of stories in the night.

Stars peek through the velvet,
The horizon deep and wide.
Nature holds its breath,
As darkness does abide.

An owl calls from the treetops,
A haunting lullaby.
The world embraces silence,
As the day bids goodbye.

A Symphony of Fading Light

Crimson hues in twilight glow,
A canvas painted bold.
Each stroke a fleeting moment,
In a story yet untold.

The sun bows with a flourish,
Casting shadows on the ground.
Nature sings its lullaby,
In a soothing, soothing sound.

Flames of gold drift gently,
Through branches high and low.
As twilight claims the sky,
To the night, we shall go.

In this symphony of light,
We find our peace at last.
Embracing the soft darkness,
As the day drifts past.

Palettes of the Departing Sun

The sun dips low with grace,
A palette rich and bright.
Swaths of orange and pink,
Bid farewell to the light.

Brushstrokes of lavender,
In the sky's vast expanse.
Colors blend and mingle,
In twilight's mystic dance.

As the world holds its breath,
In this fleeting glow,
Each hue a soft promise,
Of the night's gentle flow.

With darkness gently creeping,
The stars begin to gleam.
In the palettes of the sky,
We weave our nighttime dream.

Lasting Impressions of the Day

Sunlight spills on the green,
Painting dreams in golden hue,
Laughter dances with the breeze,
Moments held, forever true.

Whispers of the evening call,
Softly fading into gray,
Every heartbeat, every breath,
Marks the end of vibrant play.

Stars awaken in the night,
Guiding paths of drifting souls,
Memories etched in starlit skies,
Their beauty endlessly unfolds.

Time is but a fleeting guest,
Yet its touch, we still embrace,
For the echoes of this day,
Forever linger, leave a trace.

Shadowed Reflections in the Gloaming

The dusk descends, a velvet shroud,
Crimson skies make whispers low,
Shadows dance upon the grass,
As twilight paints the world aglow.

Footsteps echo on the path,
Each one holds a story dear,
Fleeting moments, softly grasped,
In the stillness, hearts draw near.

The river flows, a liquid dream,
Mirroring the secrets kept,
As stars emerge, the night unveils,
What in daylight remains swept.

In these hours, the soul finds peace,
Within the shadows, truth is shown,
For every silent, fleeting glance,
Cradles dreams we call our own.

The Warmth of an Unseen Hand

In the quiet of the night,
A gentle squeeze, a soft embrace,
Though the eyes cannot behold,
Love's presence fills the empty space.

Whispers of a long-lost friend,
Echo softly in the dark,
Though the world seems far away,
Their warmth ignites a hopeful spark.

Like a compass guiding home,
Invisible, yet oh so near,
In the silence, we can feel,
A heartbeat resonating clear.

Memories flood like summer rain,
Each drop full of laughter's song,
In the depths of solitude,
An unseen hand will guide us on.

Echoes of Luminous Farewells

The dawn breaks, whispering soft,
Colors brush the sleeping sky,
Each farewell a tender sigh,
Yet hope lingers, soaring high.

In the crowd, we wave goodbye,
Promises hang, shimmering bright,
Echoes of the times we shared,
Will follow us into the night.

As seasons change, the heart remains,
Traces of laughter, bittersweet,
In every shadow, every light,
The bonds we forged will not retreat.

With each step on this path ahead,
Carried close, each memory swells,
For in the silence of our hearts,
Reside the echoes of farewell.

Mellow Embrace of the Evening

Whispers of twilight softly sing,
The sun dips low, a golden ring.
Shadows stretch and gently sway,
As day yields night, an end of play.

Stars emerge in muted grace,
Their twinkling lights a warm embrace.
A breeze carries secrets, sweet and light,
In the mellow glow of fading light.

Quiet moments mend the soul,
In evening's calm, we feel made whole.
A touch of peace, a sigh, a dream,
In dusk's soft arms, we find our theme.

With every breath, the world slows down,
In twilight's hush, we lose the frown.
A space to pause, reflect, renew,
In evening's warmth, we rediscover hue.

Flickering Dreams at Sundown

Orange and pink paint the sky,
As dreams awaken, spirits fly.
Fleeting moments, time stands still,
Chasing sunsets, hearts we fill.

Whispers of hope drift on the breeze,
Carried by leaves of whispering trees.
With every hue, a promise made,
In dusk's embrace, our cares will fade.

The horizon blushes, soft and warm,
In this twilight, we find our charm.
Fingers grazing the fading light,
Woven dreams dance into the night.

As shadows lengthen, we hold on tight,
To flickering dreams that guide our flight.
In the tender glow, we shape our fate,
Sundown's magic, we celebrate.

The Glow of Forgotten Promises

In the twilight, memories stir,
Silent whispers, a gentle purr.
Forgotten promises, soft and sweet,
In the stillness, they find their beat.

Glimmers of hope, in shadows cast,
Echoes linger of moments past.
Through fading light, they try to rise,
A tender truth, beneath the skies.

Each heartbeat carries tales untold,
Of dreams once cherished, of love bold.
In a quiet moment, they ignite,
The glow of promises in the night.

With every sigh, we bring them near,
In the soft glow, they reappear.
A tapestry of light and refrain,
Forgotten promises, our heart's domain.

Faint Glimmers on the Edge

Faint glimmers dance on evening's cusp,
A gentle sigh, a breath, a trust.
As day gives way to starlit night,
Whispers weave with soft delight.

On the edge where shadows play,
Silent hopes drift, slip away.
Catch the flicker, hold it fast,
In the twilight, dreams are cast.

The horizon beckons, call of fate,
In the quiet, love won't wait.
A spark ignites with every prayer,
Faint glimmers shine, a promise rare.

As stars unfold in velvet skies,
We find the truth in whispered lies.
Embrace the night, let worries shed,
In the dark, we're gently led.

Dance of the Dimming Sky

Whispers through the twilight glow,
Stars awaken, soft and slow.
Moonlight weaves a silver thread,
Embracing dreams where shadows tread.

Gentle breezes carry sighs,
As night unrolls its velvet skies.
In this moment, time stands still,
Hearts entwined against their will.

Colors fade, a soft embrace,
While distant echoes leave no trace.
The world beneath a quiet spell,
In the dance where secrets dwell.

Hold this magic, let it be,
A glimpse beyond simplicity.
With every beat, the night does call,
The dance of dusk, enchanting all.

Fragments of the Sun's Farewell

Golden rays begin to creep,
Into the silence, shadows seep.
A canvas painted red and gold,
As daylight fades, stories unfold.

Whirling clouds with colors bright,
Chase the echoes of the light.
Each fragment glimmers in the air,
A moment fleeting, rich and rare.

Nature sighs, the day meets night,
As stars prepare for the first flight.
With every heartbeat, time does flow,
In these shards, the sun's warm glow.

Hold them close, these memories,
In whispers carried by the breeze.
Fragments of a day well spent,
Lost in the beauty of the moment.

The Edge of Nightfall

At the brink where day departs,
Silence tugs at restless hearts.
Shadows stretch, the colors blend,
An inkling of what dreams could send.

Fingers trace the twilight line,
Where whispers fade, and stars align.
Nature pauses, holding breath,
A moment caught between life and death.

Eclipsed horizon, soft and wide,
Harbors secrets where worlds collide.
In this quiet threshold's might,
All fears dissolve in coming night.

Cast away the day's demands,
And weave your dreams with tender hands.
Embrace the stillness, let it reign,
At the edge of night, we find our gain.

Afterglow of Dreams

In the hush where shadows play,
Lies the promise of a new day.
Echoes of what once had been,
In the twilight, soft and keen.

Flickers of hope through darkened skies,
Dance like fireflies' gentle cries.
Each dream awakes, a fragrant bloom,
In the stillness, chasing gloom.

Tender whispers chill the air,
Carrying wishes everywhere.
With every breath, the night concedes,
To afterglows of heart's sweet needs.

Hold this magic, let it stay,
In the echoes of yesterday.
For in the dark, our dreams take flight,
Guiding us through the endless night.

Soft Radiance of Dying Sun

The sun dips low, its gentle glow,
Casting shadows long and slow.
A whispering breeze, the day's farewell,
In twilight's grasp, all hearts do dwell.

Crimson hues adorn the sky,
As daylight bids a soft goodbye.
Stars awaken, shy and bright,
Embracing wings of coming night.

Golden rays melt into blue,
Nature's canvas, a vibrant view.
In moments fleeting, peace we find,
With gratitude, we leave behind.

Soft radiance, a sweet embrace,
In the hush, we find our grace.
The day now sleeps, its journey done,
In every heart, the fading sun.

Hues of the Evening's Caress

Evening drapes the world in glow,
With gentle colors soft and low.
Lavender dreams and orange sighs,
As daylight fades, the spirit flies.

Mountains wear their twilight veil,
In whispered winds, the night prevails.
Crickets sing a lullaby,
While fireflies dance beneath the sky.

The twilight paints its tender art,
A soothing balm for every heart.
In every shade, a story told,
Of moments cherished, memories gold.

As stars emerge from shadows deep,
The night unfolds, inviting sleep.
Hues of evening, calm and free,
In their embrace, we find our peace.

Twilight's Gentle Silhouette

Mountains stand in quiet grace,
Framed by dusk, a soft embrace.
Twilight whispers secrets true,
To the stars, and all anew.

Silhouettes against the glow,
Nature's magic, ebb and flow.
Every shadow holds a dream,
In the twilight's gentle gleam.

The air is thick with sweet perfume,
As flowers close, the night they'll bloom.
The sky ignites in hues divine,
A tranquil space where hearts align.

In this moment, time stands still,
As twilight paints with measured will.
A canvas vast, a soft duet,
Twilight's silhouette, our sunset.

Remnants of the Golden Hour

In the golden hour's gentle light,
Time seems to pause, holding tight.
A tapestry of rays unfold,
As day whispers secrets, soft and bold.

Fields of amber, kissed by sun,
A symphony of day is spun.
Colors dance on every leaf,
In their glow, we find belief.

The sun retreats, a final bow,
Yet linger still, its warmth allows.
Nature's palette, vivid and bright,
Remnants linger, pure delight.

Moments captured, never lose,
In golden frames, the heart imbues.
With gratitude, we softly sigh,
In the golden hour, love won't die.

Serenade of the Dimming Sky

Whispers dance in fading light,
Stars awaken, shy and bright.
Clouds embrace the evening hue,
Painting dreams in violet blue.

As shadows stretch and intertwine,
Nature hums a soft design.
The moon rises, silvered grace,
Holding secrets in its embrace.

Twilight Blossoms in the Silence

Petals close, the day is done,
Crickets sing, their lullabies spun.
In the garden, shadows play,
Twilight whispers, fading day.

Stars bloom softly, night takes hold,
A tapestry of dreams untold.
In silence, hearts begin to sway,
To the rhythm of night's ballet.

Embers of a Lost Day

The sun dips low, a crimson sea,
Flickering embers, wild and free.
Memories dance in morning's glow,
Fading shadows, soft and slow.

Each breath a whisper, time unwinds,
In the stillness, solace finds.
Lost moments shimmer, gently stay,
As twilight wraps the world in gray.

The Last Kiss of Sunlight

Beneath the arch of closing skies,
The sun descends with whispered sighs.
A golden kiss upon the land,
A fleeting touch, so soft and grand.

As night descends, the stars ignite,
The world wrapped in velvet night.
With every heartbeat, shadows race,
Embracing night's enchanting face.

Reflections of a Day's Journey

A path unfolds beneath my feet,
With whispers of the day's retreat.
The sun dips low, a golden hue,
As shadows stretch and dreams renew.

Each step a tale, each breath a pause,
I ponder life's unspoken cause.
The murmurs of the trees align,
In tangled thoughts, my heart will shine.

The rippling streams reflect the skies,
While clouds drift past in quiet sighs.
I gather moments, like soft dew,
To savor all, both old and new.

With every dusk, the stars arise,
Guiding me home with ancient ties.
In this serene, unfolding grace,
I find my truth, my sacred space.

Ephemeral Glow of the Evening Sky

The canvas glows in fiery hues,
As daylight wanes and evening brews.
A whispered breeze caresses night,
Bringing dreams, a soft delight.

The stars awaken, one by one,
Each sparkle born from day's undone.
Moonlight dances on the stream,
Cradling the world in a silver dream.

Colors shift, then gently fade,
An ephemeral serenade.
The dusk wraps close like a warm embrace,
As shadows linger, we find our place.

In twilight's glow, we pause to reflect,
On moments shared, love's sweet effect.
The sky a tapestry, vast and wide,
Holds secrets of the heart inside.

Traversing the Vanishing Spectrum

Colors blend in the setting sun,
A fleeting show, where time is spun.
Each shade a note in nature's song,
As twilight whispers, we belong.

The horizon blurs, begins to fade,
In this brief space, our dreams cascade.
With every blink, the light will shift,
Painting moments, a precious gift.

An artist's brush in cosmic hands,
Creates a world where silence stands.
We traverse paths of dusk and dawn,
In echoes where our hopes have drawn.

In the spectrum's dance, we find our way,
Embracing night, welcoming day.
Transience holds a special grace,
As colors melt in loving embrace.

The Edge of Eventide

On the brink where day meets night,
A soft glow dims, surrendering light.
The horizon blushes in tender sighs,
As stars awaken in velvet skies.

A hush falls gently, the world transforms,
In tranquil moments, our hearts conform.
The night unfolds, a vast expanse,
Inviting dreams with a silent dance.

Crickets serenade in whispered tones,
While shadows play on ancient stones.
At the edge, we linger, hearts aligned,
In the quiet, our souls unwind.

Embracing stillness, we seek the dawn,
In every echo, love's sweet song.
As twilight deepens, we draw near,
To find the magic held so dear.

Flickering Hints of Tomorrow

In the glow of dawn's first light,
Whispers of dreams take flight.
Colors bloom in gentle grace,
Hope awakens at its pace.

Across the fields where shadows roam,
Life stirs in the heart of home.
A promise lingers in the breeze,
Stirring souls with gentle ease.

Flickering through the waking skies,
Future fades, yet never dies.
Every heartbeat, every sigh,
Kisses the past as it waves goodbye.

Chasing Shadows of the Departing Day

As daylight fades, the shadows creep,
Whispers of dusk lull me to sleep.
Colors blend in twilight's sigh,
Softly bidding the sun goodbye.

Footsteps echo along the street,
Memories in silence meet.
Chasing shadows, I find my way,
In the arms of the departing day.

With every glimmer, hope still glows,
Through the darkness, courage flows.
In the night, we find our place,
With each breath, a warm embrace.

The Embrace of Evening Colors

Evening drapes the sky in hues,
Whispering secrets in gentle blues.
Stars awaken, one by one,
Painting dreams when day is done.

The horizon blushes in orange light,
A canvas born from day to night.
Breezes sigh through rustling leaves,
In this moment, my heart believes.

Each hue tells a story so bold,
Of journeys taken, laughs retold.
Crimson kisses the fading sun,
In the embrace of night we run.

Soft Footsteps of Infinite Night

The night arrives on silent feet,
Wrapping the world in shadows sweet.
Stars twinkle like distant dreams,
In the quiet, magic gleams.

Each breath stirs the stillness deep,
As the universe begins to sleep.
In the dark, our fears take flight,
Under the soft glow of moonlight.

Whispers weave between the trees,
Carried gently on the breeze.
In this realm of starry height,
I find solace in infinite night.

Glimmers of a Forgotten Horizon

Faint whispers ride the ocean's breeze,
Old tales dance under ancient trees.
Shadows play on the sandy shore,
Memories linger, forevermore.

Stars awaken, one by one,
As daylight's race begins to run.
The sky blushes in shades of gold,
Revealing secrets yet untold.

Dreams weave softly through the night,
Caught between wrong and right.
Each glimmer tells a story wide,
Of worlds that once may collide.

In twilight's embrace, we find our peace,
As the day's burdens finally cease.
Glimmers fade, yet hope remains,
In the quiet, love sustains.

The Last Breath of Daylight

The sun dips low, a final sigh,
Mountains framed against the sky.
Candles flicker as dusk draws near,
Embodied warmth, a fleeting sphere.

Crickets sing their evening song,
Natures choir where we belong.
Shadows stretch, the night unfurls,
As dreams awaken, time whirls.

The last breath hints of what's to come,
In gentle murmurs, love's soft hum.
We gather memories near the fire,
In every ember, deep desires.

Hold the twilight, cradle it tight,
Before it fades into the night.
The last breath, bittersweet, sublime,
Echoes softly, biding time.

Soft Hues of Dusk's Arrival

Colors blend as day turns pale,
Gentle whispers on the gale.
Lavender skies brush the weary ground,
In twilight's arms, we're spellbound.

Each hue tells stories of light and shade,
A palette where bright hopes are made.
The world exhales, calm in its grace,
Embracing night's familiar face.

Reflections shimmer on tranquil lakes,
Where echoes of silence softly wakes.
Memories stretch in soft silhouette,
Capturing moments we won't forget.

As dusk unfolds its tender lace,
We'll find solace in this space.
Soft hues guide us to the night,
Wrapped in dreams, tucked in light.

Twilight's Veil

A veil descends, soft and slow,
Draping the earth in twilight's glow.
Stars begin their playful dance,
Inviting hearts to take a chance.

Moonbeams weave through tangled trees,
Carrying scents of night's sweet tease.
Whispers linger, secrets told,
In the darkness, dreams unfold.

Each heartbeat echoes stories past,
Memories held, shadows cast.
With every breath, the world anew,
Twilight comforts, soft as dew.

So let us wander through this haze,
Lost in twilight's glowing phase.
Wrapped in stillness, we shall find,
The beauty waiting in our mind.

Sunkissed Memories

Golden rays dance on the sea,
Waves whisper secrets, wild and free.
Footprints trace where we once stood,
In the warmth of laughter, life felt good.

Sunsets paint the sky in hues,
Each moment cherished, we won't lose.
In a fleeting breeze, stories fly,
As time meanders, we wave goodbye.

Twilight's Wistful Caress

Shadows stretch as daylight fades,
Colors blend in twilight's shades.
A gentle breeze stirs the trees,
Whispers carried on the evening's ease.

Stars awaken, one by one,
Night's embrace has now begun.
In stillness, dreams softly weave,
Cradled in hope, it's hard to leave.

The Horizon's Final Whisper

Where sea meets sky, a soft sigh,
Fading light as day waves goodbye.
Clouds float gently, painted bright,
In quiet moments, loss feels right.

The sun dips low, a fiery glow,
In the silence, feelings flow.
Promises linger, softly spoken,
In nature's beauty, hearts unbroken.

Reflections in the Hush of Night

Moonlight drapes the world in white,
Silence reigns, the stars ignite.
Thoughts drift lightly on the breeze,
In the calm, we find our ease.

Ripples dance on the darkened lake,
Echoes of past joys awake.
In the stillness, souls connect,
While dreams and memories intersect.

The Warmth of Weightless Memories

In the hush of muted echoes,
Fragments of laughter swirl about,
Carried softly on gentle breezes,
Where sunlight and shadows dance without doubt.

Fleeting moments like whispers linger,
Soft as the touch of a feathered sigh,
Weaving tales in the loom of time,
Like stars twinkling in the vast sky.

Nestled deep in the heart's chamber,
These treasures shaped by love and grace,
A warmth that wraps around the soul,
In this sacred, timeless space.

As memories fade yet brightly shine,
They guide us through the darkened night,
In every heartbeat, in every glance,
Resides the warmth of pure delight.

Gentle Farewells to the Day

As twilight spills its golden hues,
Soft whispers greet the tired sun,
Shadows stretch as daylight wanes,
In this moment, we become one.

With every breath the night descends,
A tender hush blankets the land,
The sky blushes in soft embrace,
Anoints the earth with a gentle hand.

Nighttime's canvas, drawn in shades,
Embraces dreams that lay in wait,
Beneath the stars, a lullaby sings,
As we bid the day goodnight, sedate.

In the silence, peace is found,
As memories of day softly fade,
Gentle farewells to the day,
In stillness, our hearts are laid.

The Silhouette of Parting Light

In the waning glow, shadows play,
Sketching stories of day's retreat,
Each outline dances, graceful and free,
In the hush where dusk and silence meet.

The sun bows low in vibrant hues,
As a tapestry expands across the sky,
Fingers of dusk reach out, entwined,
With promises whispered and goodbye.

Silhouettes stand against fading gold,
Embracing the mysteries of night,
In this tranquil pause of time,
The parting light reveals hidden sights.

Within the stillness, a heart beats slow,
As evening wraps the world anew,
In the silhouette of parting light,
Before dreams take flight into the blue.

Murmurs of a Glistening Dusk

Murmurs echo as day slips away,
The horizon blushes, cloaked in mist,
Stars awaken with a brilliant sigh,
In their radiance, the night is kissed.

Glistening traces of daylight's end,
Sparkle like jewels in the cosmic sea,
Each twinkle a promise of dreams to come,
Inviting hearts to wander free.

Rippling waters catch the last light,
Whispers of nature call from afar,
In the cradle of dusk, shadows play,
Embracing the magic of each shining star.

Through every murmur, the world breathes slow,
As secrets of evening softly get shared,
In the glistening dusk, we find our place,
In this quiet moment, we feel truly spared.

The Horizon's Melancholic Glow

The sun dips low, a soft farewell,
Casting shadows where memories dwell.
Whispers of twilight embrace the sky,
Echoes of warmth as the day says goodbye.

Colors fade in a gentle sigh,
As stars awaken, the canvas nigh.
The horizon blushes, a fading art,
Melancholy strokes that tug at the heart.

Crimson bids adieu, azure takes its place,
Here in the stillness, time slows its pace.
The world holds its breath, a moment in time,
As night cloaks the day, a soft, silent chime.

In this languid hour, dreams twine and flow,
With thoughts of the past in the horizon's glow.
A bittersweet vision where hope still gleams,
In the heart's quiet chamber, we gather our dreams.

Enchanted Moments of Dimming Radiance

In the fading light of joyous days,
We wander through memory's gentle maze.
Soft laughter dances on the evening air,
As shadows merge with dreams we used to share.

Whispers of twilight caress the trees,
Gentle breezes hum like distant seas.
Each moment cherished, like dew on grass,
Evaporating swiftly, memories pass.

The sky adorned in hues of deepening night,
Stars shimmer softly, a delicate sight.
In the quiet, love's echoes softly wane,
Enchanted moments linger, yet remain.

Holding tight to what the heart knows well,
In these dimming hours, stories we tell.
Radiance fading, but never can cease,
Finding our solace in the night's sweet peace.

The Last Glimpse of Warmth

As daylight wanes, shadows creep near,
The horizon whispers secrets we hear.
A golden glow slips beneath the hill,
The last glimpse of warmth, a moment to still.

Cool winds gather, wrapping us tight,
In the rich tapestry of fading light.
We chase the sun as it sinks from view,
Holding our breath for the day to renew.

Time stretches thin, like a delicate thread,
With memories woven in hues of red.
Embers of twilight light up the day,
A promise of warmth that won't fade away.

As night draws near, we face the unknown,
Yet in this stillness, we never are alone.
For every end holds the dawn's bright kiss,
The last glimpse of warmth, a fleeting bliss.

Canvas of the Dusk

The sky unfurls in strokes of grace,
A palette of colors in twilight's embrace.
Brushes of amber, violet, and grey,
Paint the canvas of dusk, where night finds its way.

Birds quiet their songs as shadows expand,
Nature sighs softly, a tranquil command.
With each passing moment, the world withdraws,
In the canvas of dusk, we find our cause.

The stars begin to pierce the deepening hue,
Whispers of darkness cradle the view.
In this painted silence, our hearts take flight,
Finding solace within the arms of the night.

As stars emerge, and twilight holds sway,
We treasure the magic that lingers, will stay.
A canvas of dusk, where dreams intertwine,
In the stillness we seek what's eternally divine.

Echoes of the Fading Sky

Clouds drift softly in the dusk,
Whispers of colors fade to gray.
Birds take flight with an eager husk,
As night begins to claim the day.

Shadows stretch across the ground,
Footsteps fade in the cooling air.
Echoes of laughter barely found,
A memory wrapped in tender care.

Stars appear, a glowing trace,
Gleaming bright against the night.
Each a story, a secret place,
Lost within the fading light.

The sky holds whispers, soft, divine,
A canvas brushed with dreams and sighs.
In twilight's arms, our souls entwine,
While echoes linger, as time flies.

The Calm Before Darkness

The evening breathes a gentle sigh,
A hush that settles, soft and deep.
In this quiet, shadows lie,
The world awaits its time to sleep.

Stars hide behind a veil of blue,
As winds weave through the silent trees.
A fleeting moment, tranquil, true,
Before the dark, a sweet unease.

The horizon glows with amber light,
A promise of what's yet to come.
In stillness, we hold on so tight,
To the calm that makes our hearts hum.

But soon the night will take its claim,
The shadows dance, a flickered show.
We brace ourselves for the cool, the flame,
Of dreams that rise with moonlight's glow.

Embracing the Gloaming

In the gloaming, we tread so light,
A world aglow with fading fire.
The air is thick with whispered flight,
As day relinquishes its desire.

Crickets serenade the night's embrace,
With melodies that gently weave.
Stars sprinkle hope with delicate grace,
In the quiet, we learn to believe.

Each moment lingers, forever near,
As shadows dance in twilight's hue.
With every heartbeat, we conquer fear,
In this realm, all dreams feel true.

So let us gather in soft delight,
For the gloaming cradles our soul.
In its arms, we find our light,
As night unfolds, we are made whole.

Starlight's Gentle Prelude

Beneath the quilt of velvet skies,
Where stars awaken, one by one.
A symphony of twinkling sighs,
Unfolds as day's last rays are done.

The night holds secrets, vast and bright,
A prelude to each whispered dream.
In starlight's glow, we find our height,
As hope ignites like a flowing stream.

With every twinkle, tales are spun,
Of distant worlds and quiet nights.
Each pinprick shining, a story begun,
Inviting us to grasp new heights.

So come, beneath this cosmic dome,
As starlight takes us by the hand.
In this gentle night, we find our home,
In dreams that flourish, bold and grand.

Milton Keynes UK
Ingram Content Group UK Ltd.
UKHW022117251124
451529UK00012B/568